11-10

Every Day is a Gift
A MANUAL FOR LIFE

BARRY GOTTLIEB

simple truths®
THE GIFT OF INSPIRATION

Copyright © 2010 by Simple Truths, LLC

Published by Simple Truths, LLC
1952 McDowell Road, Suite 205
Naperville, Illinois 60563
800-900-3427

Design: Rich Nickel
Photos: Fotolia – pages 28, 60; iStock – pages 14, 42, 76, 98, 116, 125, 134, 139

Printed and bound in the United States of America

ISBN: 978-1-60810-062-0

02 WOZ 10

TABLE OF CONTENTS

DEDICATION

❋

To my amazing, wonderful children, Briana and Luke.
They are the two greatest gifts a man could ever hope for.
They taught me that we are born enlightened.

A note of appreciation and gratitude for all of the incredible mentors that have
had such a positive influence on my life:
Fred and Dorothy Bishop, Dr. Wayne Dyer, Zig Ziglar, Ed Forman,
Earl Nightingale, Dr. Denis Waitley, Brian Tracy, Buck Rogers, Jack Welch,
Jack Canfield, Stephen Covey, Jim Rohn, Harvey Mackay
and too many more to list here.

Special thanks to Cat Paredi, for all of her insight, wisdom, editing skills;
and for being such a wonderful partner.

I am grateful.

FORWARD

This book is designed to help you start your day off on a positive note,
and to help you overcome the obstacles that keep you from
having a great day, every day.

You don't have to read the chapters in order.
Just turn to any topic you choose ... or open to any page.
The chapters are brief and to-the-point.

Remember, knowledge is power only when you apply it.

I hope you will use the information in this book to assist you in reaching
your full potential. The best way to insure learning this useful information is
to "pass it forward." When you teach, you become the student.

Barry Gottlieb

INTRODUCTION

When I was a younger man, I lived my life with a philosophy of, "What's in it for me?" That all changed with one sentence … "You need to get your affairs in order. You have three months, six at the most, to live."

I sat across the desk from my oncologist as he spoke those words that shook my world. I thought he must be talking about somebody else.

I was diagnosed with a very rapid, fatal form of cancer. The doctor told me that there really wasn't anything they could do for it. He asked if I would be willing to try different types of experimental treatments. I figured I had no other options. The treatments made me unbelievably ill. There were many times when I thought that death would be kinder.

At the time all of this was taking place, I continued to do the best I could to live my life. My friends and family were very supportive. I had two dogs that were my best friends in the world. One was a Great Dane named Dante and the other was a German Shepherd named Zack.

Then the strangest series of events happened.

One day when I arrived home, I was shocked to find only Zack in the back yard. I had an acre of fenced yard for them to run in. The fence was five feet high, the gates were locked; but Dante was not there.

I knew no one in their right mind would try to take a 185-pound dog that was in a locked fence with a German Shepherd! The only conclusion I could come to was that Dante had leapt the fence. This was not something he had ever done before. As a matter of fact, Dante was such a good dog that if I left the gate open, he never wandered off. I started a search and could not find him.

Later that evening, I received a phone call from a trucker. He said that Dante had run into the road right in front of his 24-wheeler, and there was nothing he could do. Well, that night I sat there in my room crying. Questioning GOD about how He could take my best friend from me at a time when I was dying. I was angry with the world.

The next morning, I was getting dressed to go to the oncologist for another round of injections when the phone rang. It was the nurse at the doctor's office. She said that the doctor needed to talk to me. The doctor got on the phone and was crying; I could hear it in his voice. I thought to myself, this can't be good.

Then he said those magical, wonderful words, "You don't have cancer!" He told me that he had sent my slides and blood work to the top doctor in the world who verified that I was cancer-free.

Well, there we were, both of us crying and laughing. I thanked him for the good news and hung up, then immediately picked the phone back up to call my father. I woke him up. I told him I had good news and I had bad news. He wanted to know the good news first. I told him that I was cancer-free. He immediately said, "How could there be any bad news after hearing this?" I told him about Dante.

My father paused. I could hear him take a deep breath and he continued, "I can't believe what you just said to me. I have to tell you a story."

He told me that when he was a sergeant in the army, he had a dog and was able to keep the dog with him wherever he went. One day, the dog was missing from the barracks. He posted signs all over the base. About two weeks later, a private returned from a mission, saw the note, and went to tell my father that prior to his mission, the dog ran in front of one of the jeeps and was killed.

My father wrote home to my grandmother and told her about the loss of his dog. She wrote back and told him that she no longer had to worry about him in the war. In the village in Austria where she grew up, they had a belief that if a man was close to his dog, the dog would give its life for its master.

Wow!

My father and I cried and then celebrated our pets. Now most of you may not believe in such things. That's okay. I believe that my dog jumped that fence for a very specific reason. But this book is not about dogs and masters. It's about the celebration of each and every day. From that day forward, I made the decision to treat each day as a gift. I don't know why I was given all of these extra days. I do know that I am grateful for each and every one of them.

You do have a choice, each and every day, to have a good day; a great day!

Every day is a gift, and the quality of your life is your gift to yourself.

Barry Gottlieb

Goals

"A dream or wish
is the way we would like
the world to be.
A goal is what we intend
to make happen."

ANONYMOUS

Every day is a gift.

The vast majority of people spend more time planning their vacation or a party than they do planning their lives. As a rule, they take whatever life throws at them.

Winners, on the other hand, have learned that setting goals separates them from the mediocre.

There are three types of people in this world. People who:

1. Make it happen.

2. Watch it happen.

3. Say, "What happened?"

People who have goals, make it happen!

Goals

ACTION STEPS

※ Goals should be specific and clearly defined in writing.

※ They should be written in first person, present tense and positively [as if they already exist].

※ Identify the obstacles and challenges you will have to overcome.

※ Then, identify the resources and people you will need to assist you in overcoming those obstacles.

※ Establish a set of time frames: short term, intermediate, and long term.

- 🌞 Take immediate action!

- 🌞 Read and recite your goals every morning when you wake up, and then again prior to going to sleep.

- 🌞 Visualize your goals. See them in your mind as you recite them.

- 🌞 Be passionate and enthusiastic regarding your goals.

- 🌞 Only share your goals with positive people who will be supportive.

"Dream as if you'll live forever

live as if you'll die today."

JAMES DEAN

Garden Metaphor

"Don't judge each day
by the harvest you reap,
but by the seeds you plant."

ROBERT LOUIS STEVENSON

Every day is a gift.

When I lived in Gainesville, Florida, I had my first garden, thanks to the help and mentoring of my neighbor. Here are the lessons I learned from that experience.

Day One: Till and clean the soil. If you have never used a rototiller, it is quite an adventure.

Day Two: Go to the abandoned chicken coop, shovel the dried manure into the neighbor's truck, then return and spread it across your freshly tilled soil.

Day Three: Rototill and work the manure into the soil.

Day Four: Create rows for planting and decide what you want to grow.

Day Five: Plant the seeds. Not just any seeds, but the seeds of the crops you decided to grow.

Day Six… and Forward: Water, prune and weed.

This was extremely hard work that required planning, discipline and execution. The end result was a bountiful harvest. My garden provided me with the sweetest corn I have ever tasted, amazing tomatoes, yellow squash and delicious zucchini.

I learned some valuable life lessons from that experience. I learned that the mind is like that garden. You have a choice as to what you plant and grow.

Garden Metaphor

LIFE LESSONS

☀ Your mind is like a garden.

☀ If you plant seeds of love, compassion, truth and integrity, then you reap the rewards.

☀ If you choose not to plant anything, then weeds will overrun your garden; the weeds of hate, anger, negative thoughts and actions.

Every day is a gift.

- You must remove those weeds on a consistent basis and plant the seeds you want to harvest.

- This requires planning, hard work, discipline and execution.

- Consistent water and sun are needed.

Soar Like an Eagle

"Identify with excellence,
put your name on your work,
and both your work and your name
will stand the test of time."

DR. DENIS WAITLEY

Every day is a gift.

We have all heard the expression, "If it walks like a duck and quacks like a duck, chances are, it is a duck."

Take a good look at the people you associate with. You are probably just like them. Do you like what you see?

Are you reaching your full potential? Are you where you truly want to be in your life?

You have a choice. You can waddle and quack with the ducks, or you can choose to soar like an eagle. Do you want to be the prey, or do you want to soar free and see the world from a better viewpoint? Eagles fly free. Eagles fly high and have amazing vision. They are swift and decisive. They are majestic and proud.

If you want to soar with the eagles, you need to associate with eagles!

Are your friends pushing you to reach new heights, or are they keeping you down so they don't feel like they have to change?

Yes! You have a choice. You get to decide. Are you an eagle or a duck? YOU are responsible for the quality of your life.

Soar Like an Eagle

ACTION STEPS

☀ Give yourself a reality check-up, and take an inventory of your friends and acquaintances.

☀ Are they ducks or eagles? (Whatever your answer, the same holds true for you.)

☀ Commit to being an eagle.

Every day is a gift.

- Remember...You can't change your friends, but you can change friends.

- Surround yourself with positive role models, mentors and friends.

- Expose yourself to books, CDs and videos with positive messages.

Happiness

"There is no way to happiness.
Happiness is the way."

DR. WAYNE DYER

Every day is a gift.

In his book, *The Art of Happiness,* the Dalai Lama states that he believes man's purpose is to be happy.

Yet, we know so many people that appear to be unhappy. Recent studies indicate that 25% of the people in this country suffer from anxiety. This is an alarming number. The simple solution appears to be prescriptions for anti-depressants. But this is not a permanent solution; it is just a band-aid that provides a temporary cover up.

There is strong evidence that shows the more control we feel we have over our lives, the happier we are.

In order to feel you have control, you must begin by accepting total responsibility for YOU.

Stephen Covey, renowned author, says, "Whenever you think the problem is out there, that very thought is the problem." Yet most people continue to look outside themselves for the reasons they are unhappy. They blame their spouses, their jobs, the weather, and the list goes on. When we accept full responsibility and take total ownership of who we are, we gain control of our lives.

Responsibility = control = happiness!

Happiness

ACTION STEPS

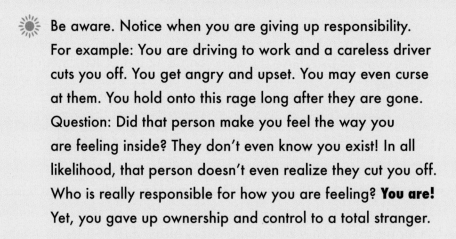

☀ Be aware. Notice when you are giving up responsibility.
For example: You are driving to work and a careless driver
cuts you off. You get angry and upset. You may even curse
at them. You hold onto this rage long after they are gone.
Question: Did that person make you feel the way you
are feeling inside? They don't even know you exist! In all
likelihood, that person doesn't even realize they cut you off.
Who is really responsible for how you are feeling? **You are!**
Yet, you gave up ownership and control to a total stranger.

☀ Take ownership. "I am responsible" is one of the most
powerful affirmations you can say. Stop giving control
to others.

- ☀ Write this affirmation down.

- ☀ Recite it first thing in the morning when you wake up.

- ☀ Recite it every time you are aware you have given up control of your life to someone or something else.

- ☀ Recite it again every evening before you go to sleep.

- ☀ No excuses! Stop blaming others and circumstances "out there," and start looking at what you can do to make positive changes in your life.

- ☀ Take immediate action!

"The only things that stand between a person and what they want in life are the will to try it, and the faith to believe it's possible."

RICH DEVOS

Someday Isle

"Remember,
you can earn more money,
but when time is spent
it is gone forever."

ZIG ZIGLAR

Every day is a gift.

I have often heard it said that one of life's greatest tragedies is when someone dies at a young age. I believe an even greater tragedy would be to live to one hundred, without ever having really lived.

Someday Isle is well known to most people. It is a place that we dream of and talk about, but where we never seem to arrive. Someday Isle is all of those things we wanted to do in our lives; all those places we wanted to visit; all those things we wanted to have. But we put them off because of "Someday I'll." Someday I'll try whitewater rafting ... Someday I'll finish school ... Someday I'll move out of this neighborhood ... Someday I'll have a family ... Someday I'll be somebody.

Think about it. What have you been putting off doing that you have always wanted to do, to have, to be? Ask yourself, what is keeping you from doing these things? Do you have limiting beliefs or fears? (See the chapters on these topics.) Are these limiting beliefs or fears real, or are they just excuses?

What if you didn't have any excuses? What would you do?

I am aware of terminally ill cancer patients that have formed "Adventure Clubs." These patients have been told they are going to die, some in a few months, others in several months, and a lucky few within the next 2-5 years.

Someday Isle

These patients started adventure clubs to seek out and do everything they were afraid to do when they were "well." They went white water rafting, sky diving, rode roller coasters and ate spicy foods they never tried before. They visited places they always wanted to see, but never made time for. They simply made the best out of every day they had left, without fear or limiting beliefs.

They would tell their loved ones they loved them, every day. They didn't hold back!

I want to share a secret with you ...

You already know this, but chances are you may have lost sight of it. Nobody is promised tomorrow. We are all going to die one day.

You don't need to have a terminal illness to decide you want to live each and every day to the fullest.

YOU have that choice today. You always have!

ACTION STEPS

☀ Remember: Every day is a gift, and the quality of your life is your gift to yourself.

☀ When you wake up each morning, TGIT (Thank GOD It's Today).

☀ Make a list of the things you have always wanted to do or try.

☀ Make a plan to start to do them immediately.

☀ Start your own club with people who want to live, not just exist, and do some of those activities together.

☀ Tell your loved ones that you love them every chance you get, and make the chances happen.

☀ Celebrate life!

Mental Fitness

"We first make our habits,
then our habits make us."

Dr. Denis Waitley

Every day is a gift.

I know if you are like most people, you make New Year's resolutions. The most common resolutions focus on changing the way you look. This is the time when most health clubs attract the majority of their members and the sale of diet-related books and videos soars.

An astonishing fact is that most new health club members stop going within thirty days. Diets are started and stopped usually within the same time frame.

Why is it so hard to keep these, and other resolutions?

Why do we do what we do, when we know what we know?

The answer is HABITS.

Yes, we are creatures of habit. Your subconscious mind stores everything, forever. So how do we overcome this hurdle?

By creating new, positive habits to replace or override the negative ones.

In order to be fit, lose weight, stop smoking, or any other resolution (or goal) you may have, you must begin by getting fit emotionally. You must begin with how you think and how you see yourself.

Mental Fitness

ACTION STEPS

- ☀ Start by getting mentally fit.

- ☀ Write your goals down. For example, write the weight you want to attain rather than the number of pounds you want to lose.

- ☀ Read your goals every morning when you first get up, and then again at night as you prepare for bed.

- ☀ Recite your goals aloud with passion and enthusiasm.

Every day is a gift.

☀ Visualize your goals as if they already exist.

☀ Everything begins with a thought.

☀ Our thoughts become our actions.

☀ Our actions, done repeatedly, become our habits.

☀ All of our habits create our character.

If there is something we would like to change about our character, we must begin by changing the way we think.

Kaizen

A MANTRA FOR HAPPINESS

"A picture may be worth
a thousand words, but a wise man
is worth a thousand pictures."

FRED BISHOP

Every day is a gift.

Kaizen (ky-zen') means *"continuous learning and growth."*

Research studies indicate that there is a direct correlation between how much a person reads and the level of success and happiness he or she achieve. Are you aware that the average American reads approximately one book each year? How many books did you read this past year? Most people make the excuse that they don't have time. Their schedules are so busy that they just can't make the time to read.

Life is all about the choices we make!

If you made the choice to get up fifteen minutes earlier five days a week, and you read something educational, inspirational, motivational or spiritual then you would literally change your life. At the end of the year, you would have successfully read 13 books. Imagine that!

You would be making a choice to make things happen in your life, rather than watch things happen. You would be in an elite group of people.

Find a mentor. Kodak has a famous saying, *"A picture is worth a thousand words."* I remember hearing this slogan one day with my dad. He turned to me and said, *"Son, a wise man is worth a thousand pictures."* He was right!

Kaizen

In this era of technology, we have access to the greatest mentors and teachers of all time, both present and past.

If you are like most people, you have a twenty to thirty minute commute to your job every morning. Why not choose to utilize this time and listen to one of these remarkable mentors? Books on CD are available in every major bookstore and most libraries, or you can purchase them online.

Imagine having mentors like Sam Walton, Jack Welch, Stephen Covey and so many others available to coach you. Wow, what an amazing way to start your day!
In addition to books and CDs, make a commitment to attend at least one seminar every year.

**Remember, a wise man or woman is worth a thousand pictures.
Seek and find mentors that will help you grow.**

Every day is a gift.

ACTION STEPS

☀ Make Kaizen your mantra.

☀ Read or listen to a book for fifteen minutes every day.

☀ Find a mentor or two.

☀ Attend seminars; get a friend to join you.

☀ Share what you learn with others. When you teach,
you become the student.

☀ Take immediate action using the knowledge you have acquired.

☀ Make learning fun and exciting.

"Wisdom is knowing
the right path to take ...
integrity is taking it."

M.H. McKee

Who Do You Work For?

"Change your thoughts
and you change your world."

Dr. Norman Vincent Peale

Every day is a gift.

"Who do you work for?" is something of a trick question. Most people have never stopped to really think about their answer. They automatically reply with the name of the company that gives them a paycheck.

I would like you to consider the following possibility.

Imagine that YOU are the Chief Executive Officer of your own company. In reality, the person you really work for is you!

Yes, that's right, you ultimately work for yourself.

Some amazing things happen when you accept this paradigm. You tend to do things differently. You take responsibility for your actions. You think differently and your performance improves.

As the CEO of your own company, you work harder to make sure that at the end of the year your company is profitable. You focus on cutting costs and expanding revenues.

You constantly look for new and better ways to improve your business, and you take ownership.

Who Do You Work For?

ACTION STEPS

- ☀ Think and act like the boss of your own company.

- ☀ Set goals for your business.

- ☀ Create a budget.

- ☀ Develop the habit of doing the things that losers don't like to do.

- Make sure that at the end of each month,
  you have made a profit.

- This means more dollars coming in than going out.

- Cut costs and eliminate waste.

- Clarity of purpose is the key to achieving your vision.

Daily Menu

"The best way to prepare for life
is to begin to live."

ELBERT HUBBARD

Every day is a gift.

Every day is a gift.

Is this statement something that you can relate to, or do you take each day for granted like most people? When you start your day, are you planning on having a great day or are you settling for whatever that day may turn out to be?

Are you aware that you actually have a choice? Yes, that's right; you have a choice whether you are going to have a good day or a bad day.

You may not be able to control the events that occur during the day, especially those events that are unexpected and challenging. But, you definitely have a choice whether you are going to allow these events to ruin your day, and how you are going to face these challenges. Most people will dwell on the challenges and allow them to get to them. They will wallow in their misfortune.

Winners, on the other hand, will look for solutions and take positive action.

We all face challenges every day. Winners deal with these challenges in a positive way. Losers see them as problems.

Daily Menu

ACTION STEPS

☀ Create the winning habit of choosing to have a great day, every day!

☀ When you first get up each morning, TGIT.

☀ Pretend you are handed a menu. On one side of the menu is a happy face with the words, "Great Day." The other side of the menu says, "Bad Day."

☀ Choose GREAT DAY!

※ Resolve that when you are faced with unexpected challenges, you are going to accept them and immediately find solutions.

※ Take immediate action!

※ Avoid replaying the challenge of bad news. Pre-play what you want to happen.

※ Move forward.

Remember ... Every day is a gift, and the quality of your life is your gift to yourself.

Limiting Beliefs

"One who fears failure
limits his activities.
Failure is only the opportunity
to more intelligently
begin again."

HENRY FORD

Every day is a gift.

Limiting Beliefs …

We all have them, yet most of us are unaware that they exist. They are keeping us from having the life that we deserve. Limiting beliefs come in all shapes and sizes. They are often masked by denial and deflection. But they are there. Most of them are not real except in our own minds.

A few of us are fortunate. We are not afraid to face them. This is the first and most important step toward making changes that will have a powerful impact on our lives and our overall well-being.

What are your limiting beliefs?

Do you think you are not smart enough, not tough enough, not pretty enough, too old, too fat, too thin? What are you afraid of? The dark, water, snakes, failure, success, public speaking, changing jobs, a commitment or something else?

Here are some action steps that will assist you in overcoming your limiting beliefs:

Limiting Beliefs

ACTION STEPS

- ☀ Identify your top three to five limiting beliefs.

- ☀ Write each one on a separate sheet of paper.

- ☀ On another sheet of paper, write a new positive belief to replace the limiting belief.

- ☀ Often, this is the opposite of the limiting belief. Better stated, it is what you are "for" rather than what you are "against." For example, a limiting belief might be stated as, "I am overweight." Change that to your new, positive belief: "I am a lean, healthy, fit and handsome man."

Every day is a gift.

☀ Your new positive belief should be written in the first person and in the present tense, as if it already exists.

☀ Close your eyes and visualize your new positive belief as if it already exists.

☀ Recite it aloud with passion and enthusiasm.

☀ Get excited!

☀ Now, take your old negative limiting belief, tear it up and throw it away. As you do this, recite, "I let it go." Immediately visualize your new, positive belief and recite it again with passion and enthusiasm.

Limiting Beliefs

- ☀ Take your time. Really get into it.

- ☀ The more visual and the more passionate you are, the stronger the picture becomes in your subconscious mind.

- ☀ For the next thirty days, recite and visualize your new positive beliefs.

- ☀ Do this when you first wake up and again before you go to sleep, every day.

- ☀ If your old beliefs try to resurface, and they usually do, say aloud, "Cancel!" and immediately replace that thought with your new positive belief.

- ☀ This requires discipline.

"The best sermons are lived, not preached."

COWBOY WISDOM

Gratitude

"Develop an attitude
of gratitude."

BRIAN TRACY

Every day is a gift.

Many years ago, I was sitting in a seminar given by Dr. Norman Vincent Peale, author of *The Power of Positive Thinking,* when a man several rows in front of me stood up to make a comment at the end of the seminar.

The man said to Dr. Peale, "All this positive thinking stuff may work for some people, but you have no idea what my problems are." The man continued, "My problems are overwhelming and you don't realize how tough I have it. I don't have just one problem. I have countless problems." Dr. Peale let the man finish venting and then he asked the man if he would like to go with him to visit a place with a population of over twenty thousand people, where not one person had a problem.

The man got very excited and said, "I would like to go there." Dr. Peale informed the man that it was just a thirty-minute drive to the Woodlawn Cemetery, and he would be happy to take him there after the seminar was over.

**The rewards in life are not given for identifying the problems.
They are given for finding the solutions.**

Be solution oriented! The most powerful technique for overcoming your problems is changing your focus. When you focus on your problems, they tend to get bigger and they seem to multiply.

Gratitude

ACTION STEPS

☀ Make a list of all of those things you have in your life for which you are grateful.

☀ Focus on the good that is already present.

☀ Focus on the abundance that you have in your life. That's right, the abundance.

☀ Look for it. You will find it! The fact that you are reading this book is a starting point for those of you who say you have nothing to be grateful for:

Every day is a gift.

- You have the gift of vision
- You can read
- You have manual dexterity
- Someone cares about you
- You have a roof overhead
- You are breathing

☀ This is just a small example of how we take things for granted.

☀ I once had a mentor say to me, "If you don't believe every day is a gift, try missing one."

☀ Change your focus.

Positive Self-Discipline

"No man is free
who is not master
of himself."

Epictetus

Every day is a gift.

Every year, Americans spend billions, yes, *billions* of dollars trying to improve themselves.

They go to seminars, read books and listen to motivational CDs that are filled with powerful, life-changing lessons.

Yet, the vast majority of these people show no discernible changes in their lives. Oh, they get excited for a brief period of time. But then they fall back into the same routine and patterns they have always had.

But, there are those few select individuals who change dramatically. They achieve the levels of happiness and success they were looking for.

How did they accomplish this? What is different about them? They read the same books. They attended the same seminars. They listened to the same CDs.

What is the missing ingredient that enabled them to achieve their desired goals?

Positive Self-Discipline

What is keeping you from having the life you deserve? The answer is really quite simple.

The key is positive self-discipline!

Positive Self-Discipline (PSD) is the key that unlocks the door and starts the engine for the life you deserve. Without this key, PSD is just theory. You must take action, consistently, in order to create permanent change.

Don't get me wrong. I am a huge fan of positive thinking and positive attitude. I give seminars on these two topics all the time. But they alone are not enough. You must take consistent action with PSD in order to create new, winning habits.

Imagine if you will, meeting Wayne Gretzky. In this meeting, Wayne explains to you how to become a hockey superstar. He shares with you all the skills and drills that have made him the best in the game. This alone will not change your game, though. I am sure you will be excited and enthusiastic. But in order to create lasting change, you must develop PSD. You must practice consistently what you have learned. You must take action.

This holds true in your personal life as well. The books and seminars are great. Now commit to taking consistent action using Positive Self-Discipline.

Time Management

"Lack of direction,
not lack of time, is the problem.
We all have twenty-four hour days."

ZIG ZIGLAR

Every day is a gift.

How would you like to get more accomplished
and feel more successful on a regular basis?
"Time management" is your answer.

Are you aware that most people have very poor
or no time management skills?

If you are one of these people, don't feel bad;
most people have never been taught these skills.
As a matter of fact, research tells us that almost
80% of Americans have poor time management
skills. I am going to share with you my "Brilliant
on the Basics" strategies for improving your time
management skills.

Time Management

ACTION STEPS

☀ To begin with, you will need the following tools: a pencil or pen and a stick 'em note pad.

☀ Step One: Before you go to bed at night, make a list of one to five things that are your priorities for the next day. Remember, the maximum amount you may list is five things.

☀ Step Two: Review your list and place them in order (top priority first). Special note: Most people get caught in the trap of doing the things that are urgent, rather than doing the things that are important. Stay focused on your priorities.

☀ Step Three: Read your list prior to going to sleep. Try to visualize the way you would like your day to go tomorrow. By doing this, your subconscious mind will actually work on these tasks while you are sleeping. It will think of ways to overcome any obstacles you may encounter the next day.

☀ Step Four: When you wake up in the morning you will have the option to change anything on your list, in case you overlooked something that is a more important priority.

☀ Finally: You have hit the ground running. You are way ahead of most people. Focus on your top priority and get it done. Do not allow anything to distract you from your mission. Scratch it off your list when completed and move on to the next priority, and so on.

☀ Do not add to your list until you have completed all of your priorities.

Your Word

"One lie ruins
a thousand truths."

GHANAIAN PROVERB

Every day is a gift.

"Do I have your word?"

Have you read the book, *The Four Agreements,* by Don Miguel Ruiz? I highly recommend it. Ruiz shares four very simple yet powerful agreements that, if followed on a consistent basis, will change your life forever.

The first of the four agreements is: "Be impeccable with your word. Speak with integrity. Say only what you mean. Avoid using your words to speak against yourself or to gossip about others. Use the power of your word in the direction of truth and love."

This is the focus of this chapter; keeping your agreements and your word. There was a time when a person's word was his bond. But today, it seems that agreements are given too often without a real commitment to honoring that agreement.

Take a good look at yourself. Are you a person of integrity? Do you honor your word? When we do not live up to our agreements, we not only lose the trust, credibility and faith of others, we learn to distrust ourselves. Our integrity and self-concept suffer. Every agreement you make, ultimately, is with yourself.

Your Word

When you realize how important your integrity and self-concept are, you will think twice before making an agreement that you do not intend to keep ... those casual agreements we agree to, like meeting somebody after work, or picking something up for a friend, or calling someone later.

These may seem like innocent agreements, but they are commitments! When we don't keep our word, we are saying more about who we are than we may realize.

When you keep your word, you speak volumes about the person you truly are. You earn the respect and trust of others.

Here are some action steps you can take on making and keeping your agreements:

Every day is a gift.

ACTION STEPS

- Pause before you give your word and say you are going to do something. Make sure it is something you intend to do.

- Write down your commitments. Use a day planner or calendar.

- If you can't keep an agreement, let the other person know immediately.

- Learn to say "No" more often.

- Remember, actions speak louder than words.

"What lies behind us, and what lies before us are small matters compared to what lies within us."

Ralph Waldo Emerson

Listen

"The true way to
soften one's troubles is to
solace those of others."

MADAME DE MAINTENON

Every day is a gift.

"The deepest hunger of the human soul is to be understood. The deepest hunger in the human body is for air. If you can listen to another person, in depth, until they feel understood, it is the equivalent of giving them air."
– Stephen Covey

One of the greatest skills we can master is the art of listening. When we listen to another person we let them know that we value them, that we care about them and what they have to say. We show them that we respect them.

Are you a good listener? Do you truly listen to others when they are speaking? Or are you caught up in thinking about how you are going to respond? Do you allow them to finish their thoughts and sentences, or are you interrupting them mid-sentence to insert your opinions?

When we interrupt people, we are in essence telling them that we are ignoring what they have to say. We are ignoring them. We are sending them a message that we don't care! This is the equivalent of an emotional slap in the face. Most of us are not even aware that we do this.

Listen

GOD gave us two ears and one mouth. We need to use them in direct proportion. This simple rule, if followed, will lead to success in all kinds of relationships, both personal and professional.

The more you listen and the better you listen, the more people will like you, trust you and want to be associated with you.

Great listeners are admired and respected. They tend to be winners. They end up at the top of their fields. They have great personal relationships.

ACTION STEPS

- Listen attentively and respectfully. Hear the person out.

- Avoid interrupting.

- Play back what you heard the person say. This is called "active listening." This lets them know that you got it; that you understood.

- Pause before you respond. Gather your thoughts.

- Practice the art of being a great listener and you will show respect, and be respected.

The Extra Mile

"It is never crowded
along the extra mile."

Dr. Wayne Dyer

Every day is a gift.

When I first started in business thirty years ago, I was taught a lesson that would prove to be one of the major keys to my success. The lesson was to do more than you are paid to do.

It seemed so simple, yet I noticed that most people did not believe in or follow this simple philosophy.

In fact, I noticed that most people had the exact opposite philosophy. I would hear people say things like, "That's not what they pay me to do," or "If they paid me more, I would do more."

I noticed that these were the same people that complained about all the things that were wrong with the company or with their boss. They would blame their lack of success on someone or something outside of themselves.

In the late '80s I attended a three-day seminar, "The Successful Life Course," presented by former congressmen Ed Foreman and his team. One of the key lessons I learned from the course was that winners

The Extra Mile

develop the habit of doing the things that losers don't like to do. The lesson was reinforced. It was clear, simple and true!

The harder you work, the luckier you get.

Author Dr. Wayne Dyer said, "It is never crowded along the extra mile."

Are you someone who consistently goes the extra mile?

Most successful people do more. They are the ones that arrive early and stay late if necessary. They think and act like winners, and they reap the rewards.

They are not there because they are smarter or more gifted. They are there because they work harder.

What can you expect if you adopt this philosophy of hard work and success? When you give more than expected, you are more likely to receive recognition and praise for a job well done.

Chances are, you will never have to worry about job security. You will create the inner characteristics of a winner. You will be well respected by your peers and by your employer.

The philosophy is easy to understand. The challenge is accepting full responsibility for yourself and for the choices you make.

Winners make it happen!

The Benefits of Failure

"My great concern is
not whether you have failed,
but whether you are content
with your failure."

ABRAHAM LINCOLN

Every day is a gift.

Yes, that's right, there are many benefits associated with failure. Most of us have never stopped to realize and appreciate the amazing and marvelous things that we have in our lives every day, thanks to those unflappable men and women who were not concerned about failure.

Look around you. Are you aware that most of the gadgets, appliances, tools, medicines and luxuries that we use were created by individuals who chose not to give up? They accepted failure as part of the learning process to achieve their objectives.

One of the greatest inventors of our time, Thomas Edison, was laughed at by his colleagues and ridiculed by the press during his attempt to bring us the electric light bulb. Edison's famous quote was, "I did not fail five thousand times to create the filament, I successfully identified five thousand ways not to."

Can you imagine the Wright Brothers giving up after one trial run? Where would aviation be today if they had not persisted?

How about Jonas Salk, Madame Curie and countless other famous doctors that gave us miracle drugs and cures?

The Benefits of Failure

Do you know the value of never giving up?

Are you aware that the greatest basketball player of all time, Michael Jordan, was cut from his high school team? Did you know that Albert Einstein didn't pass his college entrance exam the first time?

The list goes on and on. So many of the people that we have come to recognize and admire had a similar view and belief.

They did not fear failure!

On the contrary, they recognized that in order to accomplish anything new or to achieve something they had not been able to do, they had to be willing to take chances. They had to be willing to accept failure and rise above it.

Eleanor Roosevelt once said, "You can gain strength, courage and confidence by every experience in which you really stop to look fear in the face. You must do the thing you think you cannot do."

What is holding you back? What is keeping you from achieving the life that you deserve? Are you willing to face your failures, learn from them, and try one more time?

I encourage you and challenge you to be bold!

Praise

"When someone
does something good,
applaud!
You will make
two people happy."

Samuel Goldwyn

Every day is a gift.

Many years ago Ken Blanchard wrote a simple, wonderful book entitled, *The One Minute Manager.* He shared a few basic steps to assist us in becoming great managers. He told us that we should:

1) Catch people doing things right.
2) Praise people publicly.
3) Criticize only in private.

When was the last time you received praise? Think back to that moment. How did it make you feel? Now, think about the person who gave you the praise. How did you feel about him or her when they praised you?

How often do you use praise to inspire and motivate people?

Praise goes a long, long way! Yet too often we forget the value in this simple act. One of the best and easiest ways to get people to do more of what you would like them to do is to catch them doing something right or extraordinary, and praise them for what they have done.

Look for the extraordinary and the good in others and praise them for it. They will benefit, and so will you … exponentially.

Praise

ACTION STEPS

- ☀ Read *The One Minute Manager*.

- ☀ Apply what you learn in your professional and personal life.

- ☀ Be aware of how you talk with people.

Every day is a gift.

- Become an inspiring and empowering person.

- Be authentic; praise only when it is truly deserved.

- Remember…Recognition for a job well done is one of the greatest motivators of peak performance.

Fight, Flight or Freeze

"In any moment of decision
the best thing you can do is the
right thing, the next best thing is the
wrong thing, and the worst thing
you can do is nothing."

THEODORE ROOSEVELT

Every day is a gift.

When faced with danger, most people react in one of two ways. They either flee from the danger or they stand their ground and fight. This has come to be known as "the fight or flight reaction."

Over time, I have come to recognize that there is another reaction to danger: to freeze!

Like a deer caught in the headlights of a car, in this instance we do nothing. We don't flee and we don't fight. We are paralyzed by our fear, by the danger, and we freeze.

Of the three reactions to danger, I am convinced that the worse choice is to freeze.

Some of the saddest situations I have encountered have been clients or friends that are stuck (i.e., frozen) in abusive relationships. Too often, these people are so afraid that they remain in a work place or a personal relationship where there is absolutely no respect. There is constant and harmful verbal, and sometimes even physical, abuse.

Fight, Flight or Freeze

They recognize what is going on, but they are too afraid to take action to free themselves from their situation.

If you are in a work situation where you feel you are harassed or verbally abused on a regular basis, then you must take immediate action. Go to the head of Human Resources and file a written complaint. If there is no HR department, then go to a higher level of management.

If you are in a personal relationship where you feel you are not being treated with respect and you feel paralyzed and afraid to leave, seek professional help.

There are people who can help you. You are worthy. You *can* make it on your own. You *do* have a choice.

Stop being a victim!

This is the one chance we get at this life. Why would you want to spend it with someone or in a job that doesn't respect you, value you and encourage you?

> "Come to the edge," he said.
> They said, "We are afraid."
> "Come to the edge," he said.
> They came.
> He pushed them, and they flew!
>
> — *Guillaume Apollinaire*

*Remember,
as long as you live, that
nothing but strict truth can carry
you through the world, with
either your conscience or
your honor unwounded."*

LORD CHESTERFIELD

Meditation

"You must be the change
you wish to see in the world."

MAHATMA GHANDI

Every day is a gift.

If there was a way for you to be more relaxed, have less tension and anxiety, and feel more rested and full of energy, would you want to know about it? What if I told you that it only requires twenty minutes twice a day, slows the aging process and will cost you absolutely nothing?

Well, here is the answer you seek: *Meditation.*

I know that most of you have heard about meditation. Some of you may even have tried it at one time or another in your lives. But, most people have never attempted to meditate, mostly because of their misconception of what meditation is.

I often hear people say they can't imagine blocking everything from their minds (you don't have to), or that meditation requires too much training or discipline.

Here's an interesting observation: Most of you meditate and don't even realize it. For some of us it happens when we are relaxing in a warm tub, listening to music that takes us away, staring at a candle or into the fireplace, or listening to the sound of the ocean or the rain.

Science has proven that there are positive benefits to regular meditation. Here are some simple action steps that will guide you through your meditation:

Meditation

ACTION STEPS

- ☀ Find a quiet place.

- ☀ Ask not to be disturbed.

- ☀ Turn off your phone.

- ☀ Sit comfortably, with good posture.

- ☀ Choose a soothing word like love, hope, peace or a child's name.

- ☀ Close your eyes.

※ Take three slow, deep breaths. Breathe in through your nose; fill your stomach, then your chest, and breathe out through your mouth.

※ Now, breathe normally. As you do, say your soothing word aloud with each breath.

※ After a minute, say the word in your mind and continue repeating it for 20 minutes.

※ If you find your mind has wandered off, just relax and gently come back to your word.

Worry

"Whatever you
have to have,
owns you."

Dr. Wayne Dyer

Every day is a gift.

Many years ago, I was on a commercial airline "puddle jumper" from Scranton to Philadelphia. There were eight seats and we shared the cabin with the pilot and co-pilot. To make matters worse, the weather looked like something out of the Wizard of Oz. The flight was bumpy and filled with sudden drops. I was very nervous, no, make that scared!

As we approached Philadelphia, things got worse. The pilot informed us that the weather was so bad we would not be able to land until things improved.

So there I was, white knuckled, holding onto my seat for dear life. I found myself staring out the window into a solid sheet of grey clouds. I was truly afraid. I sat there looking for BIG planes to come plowing into us … as if I could change anything.

This went on for thirty minutes. My anxiety level was off the charts. I was so worried about what might occur, that the fear and anxiety grew worse and worse.

Then, out of nowhere, a story that I heard when I was in an Eastern Philosophy class popped into my mind.

It was a story about a monk who lived in a monastery that sat on a bluff three

Worry

thousand feet above the valley. Every day, the monk would go for a walk along the edge of the bluff.

One day, a hungry tiger came out of the woods and saw the monk. He started moving toward the monk.

The monk spotted the approaching tiger. He knew the tiger intended to eat him. Behind him was the valley below. In front of him was the hungry tiger.

He noticed a cherry tree growing from the side of the bluff about ten feet below the edge. The monk dropped down to the tree. There he sat, a hungry tiger and certain death above him, the valley floor and certain death below him. What did the monk do?

He ate and enjoyed the cherries!

LESSONS FROM THE STORY

☀ Worry will not change the outcome.

☀ Choose to live in the now.

☀ Live life to the fullest.

☀ Make the best of every situation.

☀ Look for the "good."

☀ Celebrate your life.

Success vs. Luck

"It's hard to beat a person
who never gives up."

BABE RUTH

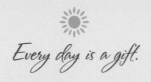

Every day is a gift.

Are successful people just lucky?

I remember, as a little boy, watching an interview on television. Gary Player, one of the greatest golfers of his time, was answering a reporter's questions. The reporter made the comment that Mr. Player was one of the luckiest golfers on the PGA Tour. Gary Player immediately responded by saying, "The harder I try, the luckier I get!"

Have you ever noticed how people in general tend to credit other people's success to luck? Do you believe this is true or do you believe what Gary Player said?

My experience has led me to believe that success is an outcome of effort and hard work, not luck.

Thirty years ago I read a book by the CEO of ITT, Harold Geneen. The one major key to success that I walked away with after reading the book was, "Do more than you are paid to do."

Success vs. Luck

On the contrary, I noticed that most people had the exact opposite philosophy. They seemed to believe that "less" was better, and they steered clear of taking initiative or venturing outside of their assigned role.

Stop waiting to win the lottery. Did you know that recent studies indicate that after three years, 68% of lottery winners are in worse financial positions than they were before they won the lottery?

Take action today to create the success and happiness that you deserve. Stop waiting for "Lady Luck" to knock on your door!

ACTION STEPS

- Believe and act like you and you alone are 100% responsible for YOU.

- Learn to give up the excuses.

- Stop blaming others for where you are in your life and for how much you earn.

- Take ownership of your actions, starting right now.

- Make hard work a habit as the condition for your success.

- Do more than you are paid to do.

- Remember...Winners develop the habit of doing the things that losers don't like to do.

A Sense of Wonder

"How old would you be
if you did not know
how old you were?"

Dr. Wayne Dyer

Every day is a gift.

My children and I had dinner at a restaurant on the beach. After dinner, they asked if they could run up and down the water's edge, and if it was okay to get their jeans wet. I responded, "Sure, go ahead." I sat and watched them as they dashed up and down the beach, playing with the incoming waves. This went on for close to thirty minutes.

As I sat there, it dawned on me that my children, as well as all children, live in the moment. They were not thinking about what happened yesterday, nor were they worrying about what tomorrow might bring. They were totally alive and living in the moment.

I thought, "What a wonderful feeling that must be."

As we grow older, we tend to lose touch with that child within us. We get caught up in replaying the past and worrying about the future. Along the way, if we are lucky, we have a few brief instances of living in the moment.

That child is still there, inside all of us. We need to keep that sense of wonder alive. We need to understand that it is okay to dance in the waves, to sing outside of the shower.

To live!

A Sense of Wonder

ACTION STEPS

☀ Take a child out for the day, even if you have to borrow one from someone you know.

☀ Play hopscotch with your neighbors, both the adults and the kids.

☀ Get some crayons and a coloring book...Draw outside the lines.

☀ Go to the park and fly a kite.

☀ Play in the rain and jump in the puddles.

☀ Ride roller coasters and eat cotton candy.

☀ Lie in a field, look up at the clouds and figure out the shapes.

☀ Keep the child within you alive…
Go ahead…I dare you!

"The optimist sees opportunity
in every danger;
the pessimist sees danger
in every opportunity."

WINSTON CHURCHILL

True Abundance

"If you want others to be happy,
practice compassion.
If you want to be happy,
practice compassion."

THE DALAI LAMA

Every day is a gift.

What does "True Abundance" mean to you?

According to Wikipedia, the definition of abundance is "the opposite of scarcity."
I believe true abundance is not measured by what you have; rather, it is measured by
what you give.

In our culture, it seems that most people are caught up in their "need for greed."
Perhaps this is why so many people struggle to find their happiness, and why over
25% of the people in our country suffer from anxiety. We live in a culture where we
are taught to judge a person based on what they have, rather than on who they are
and what they contribute to society.

I was very fortunate to have met a professor that changed my whole way of thinking.
I was one of those people with a, "What's in it for me?" attitude when I started
his class. By the end of the semester though, my philosophy and my attitude had
changed. Forever! This is what I learned:

"You can have anything you want in life, if you will just help enough
other people get what they want." *- Zig Ziglar*

I challenge you to focus on this philosophy for an entire month! Here are some action
steps that will help you stay focused on this incredible gift:

True Abundance

ACTION STEPS

- ☀ Gratitude. Every night before you go to sleep, recite aloud at least ten things for which you are grateful.

- ☀ Forgive. Let go of the past. Forgive those who have hurt or angered you. Stop carrying this poison around with you every day.

- ☀ Love. Be sure to tell those people in your life who mean so much to you that you love them and appreciate them.

☀ Donate. Go through your closets. Anything you haven't worn or used in the past year, box it or bag it and take it to a place where those who are less fortunate will benefit from your donation. Get your children involved!

☀ Praise. Make time to praise. Look for and recognize the good in others.

What Makes a Champion?

"The will to win is important,
but the will to prepare is vital."

JOE PATERNO

Every day is a gift.

Have you ever stopped to reflect on what makes a true champion? How did they get there? What makes them so special? Are they born that way? Is it in their genes, or is it skill?

If you look at the best teams in the world and the greatest individual champions, you will find that they have two characteristics that separate them from the average person or team.

First, they train on a regular, on-going basis. Second, they have mastered the skill of pre-playing the outcome of events long before they actually perform them.

In a nutshell, these outstanding individuals and teams are brilliant on the basics. Whether it is a professional sports team or an astronaut, each spends countless hours preparing, both physically and mentally, for the tasks before them.

These same qualities make companies and individuals successful. Yet recent studies indicate that up to 80% of companies do little or no training, other than product training, on a regular basis.

How about you? Are you doing the things that champions do? Are you brilliant on the basics?

What Makes a Champion?

ACTION STEPS

☀ Start by making the choice to be the best you are capable of being.

☀ Create the habit of regularly scheduled training.

☀ Visualize the outcome you desire in your mind, and pre-play it over and over again until it becomes automatic.

☀ Study other champions. Learn how they mastered their skills.

Staying Youthful

"Do not regret growing older.
It is a privilege denied to many."

UNKNOWN

Every day is a gift.

Men and women have been searching for the secret
to eternal youth since the beginning of time. My first
recollection of it was in the fourth grade, when I read about
Ponce De Leon and his quest for the fountain of youth.

Every single day you hear about another product or
gimmick that is going to help you look young, stay young
and feel young. Sometimes, the pressure to be youthful is
too overwhelming.

Billions of dollars are spent each year on lotions, pills,
surgery and other "solutions" to stay young and vibrant.

I would like to offer some alternative solutions for staying
youthful. After all, youth is a state of mind.

Staying Youthful

ACTION STEPS

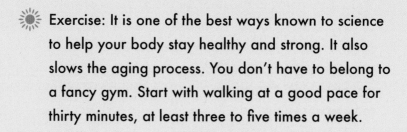

- Exercise: It is one of the best ways known to science to help your body stay healthy and strong. It also slows the aging process. You don't have to belong to a fancy gym. Start with walking at a good pace for thirty minutes, at least three to five times a week.

- Time for you: Set aside a minimum of thirty minutes just for you, every day. Do something you are passionate about. Make this a habit.

Every day is a gift.

☀ Positive people: Beware of the energy vampires.
Take a good look at the group of people that
you associate with and that you call your friends.
Spending time with positive people will have a
positive impact on your well being.

☀ Enjoy simple things:
Sunsets … clouds … walks … trees … butterflies …
good music … good food … deep breaths … life!

☀ Remove stress: Let go of guilt … meditate …
enjoy yoga … sing … dance … laugh … love!

Respect

"Whenever you
judge someone else,
you do not define them,
you define yourself."

STEPHEN COVEY

Every day is a gift.

My father dropped out of school when he was in the eighth grade, but he managed to acquire a Ph.D. in street smarts. He was one of my greatest mentors. One of the best lessons I learned from him was the following, "Don't judge a man by the way that he treats the president of a company; judge him by the way he treats the janitor of the company."

My Pop was right!

Everyone deserves to be treated with respect.

This should be one of the core values of your family and of your business. Respect starts with you. If you don't respect yourself, you will find it very difficult to respect others. Remember: when you command respect, people will gladly follow you. When you demand respect, they will work against you.

Respect

ACTION STEPS

- ☀ Praise publicly.

- ☀ Criticize privately.

- ☀ Look for the good.

- ☀ Catch people doing things right and praise them for it!

- ☀ Let people know that you genuinely care.

※ Separate the person from the action.
Let them know it is the action that you
do not approve of, not them.

※ Be candid and sincere.

"There is no sudden leap to greatness. Your success lies in doing, day by day."

Max Steingart

Knowledge Is Power

"If you want to be successful
and happy, you need to
spend more time working on you,
than you do on your job."

JIM ROHN

Every day is a gift.

"Knowledge is power!"

Is this a true statement? Does knowledge really give us power?

The answer may surprise you.

Even though we have heard the statement over and over again, it is not true. Knowledge is only powerful when you use it! Think about it. If the Surgeon General told us that smoking causes cancer, would that knowledge give us power? I hope so, but only if we use it! We have access to almost unlimited information and knowledge. Yet only a small percentage of us use that knowledge to empower ourselves and others. Enrich your life and that of others.

Take your knowledge and use it for a positive purpose!

Knowledge Is Power

ACTION STEPS

☀ Read something inspirational, educational or spiritual every day.

☀ Attend at least one seminar every year.

☀ Teach what you learn to others. Whenever you teach, you become the student.

☀ Turn your knowledge into power by taking consistent action.

☀ Remember...Perfect practice makes perfect.

Every day is a gift.

Beware of Negatrons

"Winners develop the habit
of doing the things that losers
don't like to do."

ED FOREMAN

Every day is a gift.

Who or what is a "Negatron?"

You can find them at work, at play, at social events, really almost anywhere you go. Negatrons are people that focus on the bad, the negative, the worst of times.

They are the people that like to criticize, condemn and complain. They like to suck you into their world of apathy and mediocrity.

They do all they can to keep you from moving ahead. They are intent on keeping you down because it makes them feel better knowing they are not alone.

They follow the belief that "misery loves company."

Negatrons want you to work less, try less and achieve less! They are this way because it makes them feel better to know there are others just like them, who always choose the path of least resistance.

YOU are better than this!!!

Beware of Negatrons

ACTION STEPS

- ☼ Steer clear of Negatrons!

- ☼ Take an inventory of the people you choose to spend time with. Are they winners?

- ☼ Make sure your friends and colleagues build you up, rather than put you down or shut you down.

Every day is a gift.

- ☀ Be a positive influence!

- ☀ Build a positive peer group that takes you to new heights.

- ☀ Find mentors and coaches that help you achieve your true potential.

Five Gifts

"Try not to become
a man of success,
but a man of value."

ALBERT EINSTEIN

Every day is a gift.

One of my favorite seminars is titled, "The Five Gifts." I love sharing this seminar because it is all about YOU giving yourself five simple gifts that will change your life forever.

What follows is an abbreviated version of "The Five Gifts."

Gift 1: Use the first hour after you wake up doing something positive. No television. No radio. No newspaper.

Gift 2: Spend thirty minutes prior to bedtime reading, listening to or viewing something positive. No negative media or stimuli.

Gift 3: Give yourself thirty minutes to an hour every day, doing something just for you. Choose something you want to do and make it happen. No excuses!

Gift 4: Spend two to five minutes each day recognizing and acknowledging your accomplishments for the day. Pat yourself on the back!

Gift 5: Set aside five to ten minutes each day to reflect on the many things you have in your life for which you are grateful.

Make these "gifts," habits!

Expectations

"Seek first to understand,
then to be understood."

STEPHEN COVEY

Every day is a gift.

My experience as a business/life coach and as a business owner has taught me that one of the greatest sources of frustration for leaders and managers is caused by their expectations.

We continually expect the people who work with us to do things the same way we would ... to do them with the same level of intensity, passion, and to achieve the same results we would have, had we done them ourselves. The end result is usually one of disappointment and frustration for both parties.

The truth is, it is unrealistic to expect that everyone is going to do things the same way that you would.

We are all different and unique. Our experiences and education, along with our training, are all going to be at different levels. Our level of passion depends on our individual beliefs, desires and personal histories.

Great leaders take people from where they are and help them grow.

Our personal relationships hold similar challenges and solutions. Celebrate the differences and find strength in them.

Expectations

ACTION STEPS

- ☀ Accept people (including yourself) for who they are and what they are capable of.

- ☀ Allow them to grow and improve at a reasonable pace.

- ☀ Encourage and support them in their efforts.

- ☀ Remember... Great communication is a key ingredient in improving any relationship.

- Be patient.

- Be tolerant.

- Be understanding.

- Be accepting.

- Be firm, but fair.

- Remember...Clarity is the key!

- Look for the good; catch others doing things right and praise them for it.

Your Core/Your Integrity

"Begin with the end in mind."

STEPHEN COVEY

Every day is a gift.

Having a clear picture of who we are and what we want is something that most of us don't stop to think about. We start and end our days without giving much thought to whether or not we are on the path we should be on. Most of us lead our lives without giving much thought to our true purpose or intentions. We end up trying to live the lives that the marketing and advertising companies misguide us into believing we should be living.

The end result is a society of people that are out of balance and out of touch with what really matters to them and to others. We spend so much time trying to be something and someone other than who we really are.

Setting goals regarding where you want to get in life or who you want to be is a good start.

But, if you don't begin with who you are and where you are, it will be difficult for you to set a course for your desired outcome. You must begin by looking inward to understand who you are and what your core values and beliefs are. Only then will you be able to chart a course for the life that you deserve.

Your Core/Your Integrity

ACTION STEPS

- ☀ Give yourself a check-up from the neck up.

- ☀ Write down your core values and beliefs.

- ☀ Share them with your loved ones.

- ☀ Ask yourself if you are living a life consistent with these values and beliefs.

- ☀ Create a picture in your mind of what you want, and who you want to be in your life.

Every day is a gift.

- ☀ Live the vision.

- ☀ Set clear goals that are consistent with your core values and beliefs.

- ☀ Celebrate your accomplishments.

- ☀ Acknowledge and be thankful for everything for which you feel you should be grateful.

Forgiveness/Letting Go

"GOD grant me the serenity to accept the things I cannot change; courage to change the things I can; and the wisdom to know the difference."

REINHOLD NIEBUHR

Every day is a gift.

What are you holding on to?

We have all been there: someone or something has impacted our lives in a negative way, and we can't seem to let it go. We hold on to the event, replaying it over and over again in our minds. In doing so, we only make matters worse. This is like throwing gasoline on a fire in an attempt to put it out.

We use up vital energy by continuing to replay the event.

The fact is, there are no "woulda, coulda, shouldas." We can't change the past, no matter how hard we wish we could. All the replays in the world will not undo what has been done.

We do have a choice, though. A choice regarding how we want to deal with what happened. We have the opportunity to take our energy and apply it in a way that helps us move forward, that helps us heal.

We can learn and grow from what has happened. We can use that energy in a positive way. If we hold on to the negative, then we continue to allow that event to own part or all of us. When we make the decision to let go or forgive, we take back the power we have given away.

Forgiveness/Letting Go

ACTION STEPS

- ☀ Make a list of the negative people or events that you are holding on to.

- ☀ Be aware of how these people or events make you feel.

- ☀ Look for the lesson that you can learn from what has happened and write it down.

- ☀ Recognize that replaying the event will not change what happened.

Every day is a gift.

- ☀ Repeat aloud, "I let it go."

- ☀ Resolve to never let it happen again.

- ☀ Affirm aloud the way you want your life to be, and who you want to be.

- ☀ Take back control/ownership of your life.

ABOUT THE AUTHOR

Barry Gottlieb

FOUNDER: Coaching the Winner's Edge organization and coaching program / *www.barrygottlieb.com*

BUSINESS BUILDER: Built a $75 million international company in twenty-two years.

COACH: Both a life and a business coach with a successful practice offering counsel and guidance to individuals and major corporations.

AUTHOR: *Brilliant on the Basics,* which focuses on real people, real stories, and real lessons (soon to be released).

RADIO HOST: Co-host of "the Success Show," a one-hour talk radio program broadcast weekly in South Florida.

SPEAKER AND TRAINER: Inspires, coaches and trains through programs for both large and small audiences and corporations.

SALES EXPERT: Former VP of Sales for a billion-dollar corporation.

NEWSLETTER PUBLISHER: Founder/Publisher of the "TGIT"(tig'-it) weekly newsletter www.tgit.org.

WEBISODE HOST: Co-host of "The Insight," a half-hour weekly broadcast that deals with effective change, positive thinking, holistic health, and many other topics dealing with transformation. Available at *www.BocaRaton.com.*

If you have enjoyed this book we invite you to check out our entire collection of gift books, with free inspirational movies, at **www.simpletruths.com.** You'll discover it's a great way to inspire **friends** and **family,** or to thank your best **customers** and **employees.**

The
simple truths®
DIFFERENCE

Our products are **not available in bookstores ... only direct.** Therefore, when you purchase a gift from Simple Truths you're giving something that can't be found elsewhere!

For more information, please visit us at:
www.simpletruths.com Or call us toll free... 800-900-3427